Invent[illegible] Good Thing Leads To Another

by Hiro Takahashi
Illustrated by Bruce Day

Editorial Offices: Glenview, Illinois • Parsippany, New Jersey • New York, New York
Sales Offices: Needham, Massachusetts • Duluth, Georgia • Glenview, Illinois
Coppell, Texas • Sacramento, California • Mesa, Arizona

Have you ever heard about an amazing new invention? You might say, "Who thought of that wonderful idea? That person is a genius!"

Inventors are amazing people. They think outside the box. They work hard at something for a long time. Their names go down in history.

Where do inventors get their ideas? Often, an invention starts with an idea someone had a long time ago.

---

outside the box: differently from other people

go down in history: are remembered for a long, long time

Let's look at the invention of the lever, for example.

Some time back in the past, hunters used poles to lift a heavy animal onto a skin and drag it home.

Another person thought of a way to lift a friend to pick fruit.

Such things probably happened hundreds of times—all over the world. All these prehistoric people used levers. We just don't know what they called their "invention."

---

prehistoric: long, long ago, before people wrote things down

Many hundreds of years after prehistoric people first used levers, a Greek man wrote about them. He understood what they could do, and he taught other people how to use them. The man's name was Archimedes (ark uh ME deez), and he lived about 2,200 years ago!

Because Archimedes described this simple tool, he is sometimes called the inventor of the lever. He was not the first person to use a lever, but his explanations helped others find new ways to use it.

Levers work by pushing or pulling. A person pushes down one end of the lever, and that effort lifts or moves a load on the other end. Here, the gardener pushes vigorously (the effort) on the shovel (the lever), and the other end of the lever lifts the dirt (the load).

A pair of scissors has two levers attached at a fulcrum in the middle. Pull the handles apart, and the sharp ends of the lever move apart. Push the handles together, and the sharp ends move together. The sharp ends of the lever (the blades) cut the paper.

---

vigorously: in a strong way

fulcrum: the support on which a lever moves

The lever might seem simple today. But this simple machine is part of thousands of later inventions, including simple ones like scissors and not-so-simple ones like pianos. One good thing leads to another.

Look inside a grand piano. There are many levers. Your finger provides the effort. That effort pushes a piano key (one end of a lever) down. As the other end of the lever raises up, it pushes up another lever (the load). Inside the piano, levers keep pushing or pulling one another until finally, a soft, little hammer (another lever) strikes a wire. Wow! You have music!

wire

hammer strikes wire

finger pushes key down

levers raise up

Let's take a look at another invention: the personal computer or PC. Today, scientists use PCs to do difficult math problems. Who invented the PC? Let's start at the beginning. To do that, we need to go back 5,000 years!

Even 5,000 years ago, people used math. A farmer needed to know how many crops to trade for a sheep. A peasant, or poor farmer, needed to know how many bricks to use for a wall.

In Babylonia (modern-day Iraq) people dug lines into sand or dirt and put pebbles in them. They did calculations by moving pebbles from one line to another. This worked well, unless a dust storm blew the sand away.

---

pebbles: very small rocks

Eventually, someone thought of making a calculating device that the wind wouldn't blow away. The abacus (A buh kus) was invented. Who invented it? We don't know. People used an abacus in Egypt about 2,500 years ago. A little later, it was used in China, and it is still widely used there today.

An abacus has beads on sticks or wires inside a frame. You do calculations by moving the beads.

The Aztecs in Mexico used an abacus sometime around the year 900. Their abacus used dry corn instead of beads.

Extend Language **Context Clues**

Context clues help you learn the meaning of a new word. Context clues are the other words and sentences surrounding a word. Context clues may be in the same sentence, in the same paragraph, or in the same article.

Read pages 7 and 8 again. Look for context clues for the word *calculations*. What does the word *calculations* mean? How did the context clues help you learn the word's meaning?

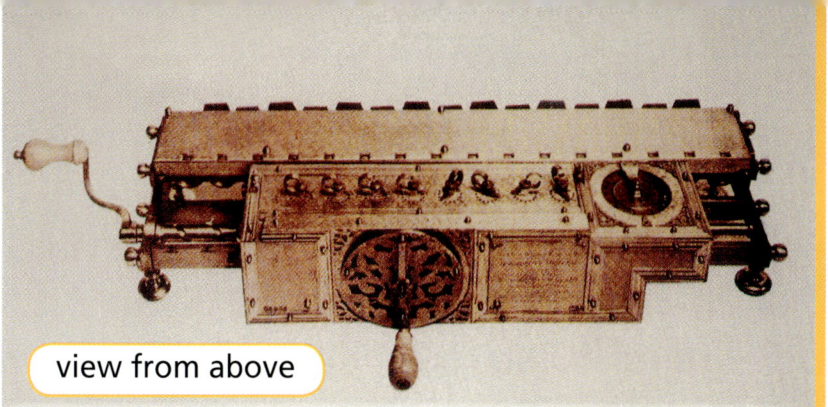

view from above

Calculating machine, invented in Germany by Gottfried Wilhelm Leibniz in 1671

view from below

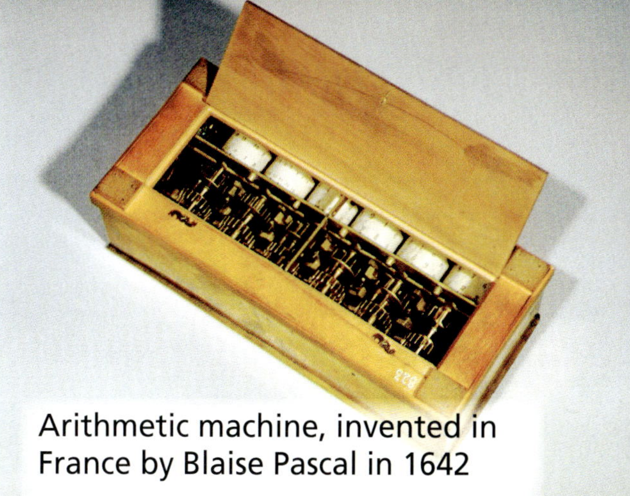
Arithmetic machine, invented in France by Blaise Pascal in 1642

In the 1600s, people invented new kinds of calculators. These inventions were quite different from the abacus. And each new calculator was more powerful than the earlier one. These early calculators helped pave the way for computers.

---

pave the way for: prepare people for

The first true computer, called ENIAC, was finished in 1946. It filled a whole room.

The first true computer was built for the United States Government in 1946. It was so big that people could walk around inside it! And they had to, to make it work.

By the 1970s, computers were small enough to pick up and carry. Today, most schoolrooms and homes in the United States have computers.

People will tell you that computers were invented in the late 1900s. Actually, the invention took more than 5,000 years! It took time, but one good thing did lead to another.

Many things have their roots in earlier inventions or earlier ideas. Let's look at one more example. Today, many people wear contact lenses to improve their sight. Adolf Eugen Fick invented them in 1887, but there's more to the story. Look at this time line.

1000	Pieces of glass were set on written words to make them look bigger
1508	Leonardo da Vinci draws pictures of the idea of contact lenses in Italy
1636	René Descartes draws pictures of contact lenses in France
1262	In England, Roger Bacon experiments with lenses to make things look bigger
1268–1280	Alessandro di Spina introduced eyeglasses in Italy, but they were used in China at this time, too
1784	Benjamin Franklin invents bifocal lenses in Massachusetts
1887	Adolf Eugen Fick fits contact lenses on animals and people in Germany
1970s	Soft contact lenses are invented in the United States

---

have their roots in: come from; were inspired by

bifocal lenses: two-part lenses with one part for reading and one part for seeing far away

Inventions make our work easier. Sometimes, they change the way we live. Everything from levers to contact lenses, from shovels to computers, from scissors to grand pianos was invented. Almost every time, the inventor built on earlier ideas. One good thing led to another.

What would you like to invent?